Rainbows, Butterflies & One Last Hug

A Mother's Spiritual Journey Losing
Two Children to Cystic Fibrosis

PEGGY S IMM-ANESI

BALBOA
PRESS

A DIVISION OF HAY HOUSE

ISBN: 978-1-4525-6102-8 (sc)
ISBN: 978-1-4525-6104-2 (hc)
ISBN: 978-1-4525-6103-5 (e)

Library of Congress Control Number: 2012922811

Balboa Press books may be ordered through booksellers or by contacting:

Balboa Press
A Division of Hay House
1663 Liberty Drive
Bloomington, IN 47403
www.balboapress.com
1-(877) 407-4847

Because of the dynamic nature of the Internet, any web addresses or links contained in this book may have changed since publication and may no longer be valid. The views expressed in this work are solely those of the author and do not necessarily reflect the views of the publisher, and the publisher hereby disclaims any responsibility for them.

The author of this book does not dispense medical advice or prescribe the use of any technique as a form of treatment for physical, emotional, or medical problems without the advice of a physician, either directly or indirectly. The intent of the author is only to offer information of a general nature to help you in your quest for emotional and spiritual well-being. In the event you use any of the information in this book for yourself, which is your constitutional right, the author and the publisher assume no responsibility for your actions.

Any people depicted in stock imagery provided by Thinkstock are models, and such images are being used for illustrative purposes only.
Certain stock imagery © Thinkstock.

Printed in the United States of America

Balboa Press rev. date: 12/5/2012

MY DAUGHTER MEG ANESI (NO FEAR)

BORN 9/1/1973

DIED ON MOTHERS DAY 5/12/2002 FROM

CYSTIC FIBROSIS

In Loving Memory of My Daughter
Margaret Grace Anesi

My Special Angel

When you smiled, you could have lit the night sky
I still don't understand why so young you had to die
Guess the Lord must have needed you up there
Amongst the stars and angels,
Sometimes life isn't fair.
I am sure that Heaven is a better place since you arrived
You are now free to breathe above rainbows high in the sky
With freedom to fly above the clouds
like all of the butterflies.
All I asked for was one last hug. Then, I
would bottle it in the world's largest jug.

I will love you "forever"
-Mom

Dedications:

To my niece, Melissa Imm, the editor who made this book possible. To my daughter Meg: I will love you forever until we meet again. To my friend Karen Keller-Zedda and her kids, especially her daughter Elaine Zedda-Palmaffy, who were always there to throw me a life preserver when I felt like I was going to drown in my sorrows and also to her kids who made me feel special on Mother's Day knowing how tough that day is on me. To my friend Carol Moran who has been my spiritual strength and believed in me. She gave me the push I needed to write and also introduced me to a medium named Deborah Hanlon who reached beyond life and into the afterlife. Deborah brought through my parents, brother, sister, and daughter and son and estranged husband (who all passed away within the past decade). Intuitive Medium Deborah: Thank you so much for everything and helping to keep my sanity. To my very good friend Sabrina and the late Chuck Reilly: You were both there for me so many times and on the night of my sister's death (after we accidentally bumped into each other after you attended a tag sale), Sabrina picked up a silver butterfly hairpin and didn't know why and felt the need to give it to me for some reason without even knowing the importance of the butterfly. I know there was a deeper meaning behind this generosity. To Kathy Herde: thank you for always being there and for thinking of me after each of my loved one's deaths. To Alison Kurie: you pushed me back into reality when I sat in the dark for weeks behind closed blinds after my daughter's death on Mother's Day (May 12, 2002). Christine Dillon: who always made me laugh. To my friend Betty Williams whom I've known since we were fifteen years old and has been through a lot of my bumpy paths and helped me to smooth them out. Martin D: you stood by me as a friend for many years. To my grandchildren Amber and Chris Pinter: I love you. To Colleen S who helped me on many occasions before and after my daughter's death and who was by my side when my son took his last breath. To those whom I have lost: Pat Bouton (my sister), Ellie Imm (my brother), and to my Mom and Dad. And since I wrote this book while working on my next, my late husband Don the father of my children who also passed away 9 months before my son I love you all! Last but not least, my two sons, Don and Dan, who put up with me and shared my pain. To my siblings, Lee Imm, Bob Imm, and Mary Imm Carlucci who were there for me, and John Edwards Medium from the show Cross-Country which made me a believer in Mediums. To Christine Nester and Tracey Powell-Lynch: thank you for being like daughters to me! To my youngest son Marc, who has now passed since I finished this book and shared the same fate as his sister, Mommy loves you all. Thank you to Kathy Brophy, my grandchildren's paternal grandmother for all of her support and all that she has done during my daughter's life and after. Thank you to Pat and Ted Oswald from Verplanck, who I worked for during and for a while before and after my daughter's death for being like family to me and letting me work around my daughters illness you guys are very special to me. Thank you to my best friend and companion, Tommy Cordts, who stood by me through it all.

MY LATE CHILDREN MEG AND MARC 1989 AT SEASIDE NJ

PEGGY S. IMM-ANESI

Biography:

Peggy is a woman who grew up in a small town called Croton-on-Hudson, NY. It is located 30 miles North of NYC in the beautiful upper Westchester County. Croton is known for The Croton Dam (Croton Gorge)which is the second largest hand-hewn structure in the world, with the first being the pyramids in Egypt, and was also home to many famous people over the years including Jackie Gleason (The Honeymooners) and Allen Funt (Candid Camera) to name a couple. There are so many more famous people from Croton whom she has also named in her book. Peggy got married in 1972 to another Croton person, Donald Anesi, whose family also played a big part in building the town into what it is today, as both of their families have lived there since the late 1800's. They had 4 children, three boys, Donnie, Danny, and Marc, and one girl named Meg. Their oldest and youngest were born with the genetic illness, Cystic Fibrosis and passed away while in their twenties. She now lives about 4 miles North of where she grew up, on a piece of land with the most breathtaking view of the Hudson River in Verplanck, NY. She started writing a few years back as a way of venting and keeping notes of what she was feeling and decided that she had a book here. This book could help other people who are grieving, since we have all lost loved ones, and she has lost so many in a very short time including both parents, a brother, a sister, brother-in-law, sister-in-law, two children, husband, and the list goes on. Peggy thinks she can help so many by sharing her life story especially people who have lost a child as she has lost two children, a daughter and son to Cystic Fibrosis. Her daughter Meg died on May 12, 2002 on Mother's Day of all days. Nine months before her son Marcus died on February 2, 2011 her husband died on April 22, 2010. Though Don and she were separated, she also took care of him at the same time while also caring for her dying son. Her other two sons, Don and Dan lost 3 generations in about 9 months as their paternal grandfather, Donald also died on August 26, 2010. Of course her books are real life but touch on many other subjects such as spirituality and the true life experiences she encountered since her families deaths, including some very strange happenings. Her goals are now to sell her books, to work on her second book "Racing Honda's in Heaven"(as these books can help pay off bills because she still owes so many now due to illness and deaths). Plus, she suffers from her own illness, Multiple Sclerosis, but keeps on going the best she can. She wants to help other families with sick children because there are so many things they need help with that people don't understand. Only someone who has been there could relate to them. Parents with sick children need money to eat while at the hospital and for car parking fees as they add up (especially in the city where it can cost $35 a day) and not everyone has that kind of money to spend. Also, many cannot get life insurance due to the nature of some illnesses so she would like to help them with their final expenses. Peggy will start a foundation in memory of both of her children which will be called "*The Meg and Marcus Anesi Children's Foundation* "and will start by letting people know what the needs of these families are so together they can make life easier for these people who are already going through enough without worrying about other things that most take for granted. She has been there and she knows how hard it can be so she will take what affected her family the most in their journey thus far and turn the negative into positive through their life lessons.

ST. MARY'S CHURCH IN SCARBOROUGH

(WHERE MY DAD, ELLSWORTH IMM WORKED)

Loving The One Who Never Left Me

Written by Peggy S Imm-Anesi

I am reminded once again if there is one thing
in life I can count on it's the Lord above
He is still there for me and makes me feel
pure like the morning dove.
There are things in life I have done that I am not so proud of
But he heals me through his truth and his unconditional love.
When others have turned their back and have let me down
He throws me a life preserver so I will not drown
As there were times I could have filled a river
with all so many tears I have cried
Especially when I lost my two children, Meg
and Marc, on the day they died.
But now, I will hold my head up high as I
have been given back my pride
As now my books are coming out and chapters
of our lives will finally be told
Then I will finally have peace in my life as I am now growing old.
I hope when you read the story of our journey
and the things we have done

Though life is all so very hard at times but God
still starts each day with the morning sun
Just one more thing to think of some food
for thought through all our pain
There would never be a rainbow which is
God's promise without some rain.

Introduction:

First, I would like to thank all of my friends and family who have stood by me and have encouraged me to finally write this long, overdue book. I've been talking about it for a while but now it has finally become a reality. This book is an account of recent and past events in my life from both a personal and a spiritual perspective. I believe we all have a calling in life and now this seems to be mine. Though writing can be therapeutic for the writer, I also believe that I will be able to reach many other people who have had similar experiences and let them know that they are not insane and they are not alone. Thanks again to all of those who inspired me!

Chapter 1

MY LIFE AS A CHILD

WITHOUT SOUNDING SELF-ABSORBED, I GUESS I should start at my own beginning. I was born on September 7th, 1953 during a hurricane. I was the fifth of six children to a blue-collar worker and a stay-at-home mom (the traditional dysfunctional family). I guess even when I was very young, I knew I needed to bring something more to the world around me.

When I turned 3, I was referred to as "quite the little actress" because I was always singing and dancing with thumbtacks in the bottoms of my Sunday-school patent leather shoes. I would always dance with pride on the wooden floors of our home. My parents didn't have the money to provide me with real tap shoes. My dad worked on the railroad during the day and during the nights and weekends, he worked at our church cleaning and as a groundskeeper (known as a sexton). Quality time with my father would be about half an hour a night spent in the basement of our home where I would sing along as he would play the accordion and the violin. I credit him for my love of music and dance.

Growing up with 5 other siblings could be rough at times. When my youngest brother, Lee was born in 1956, we ranged in ages from newborn to twenty years old. By having that many kids, money was tight in our family. Soon, my older brother and sister would marry, at which time I was about to enter school...but of course not to each other...lol! My older brother got married first to his wife Marilyn and soon to follow in his footsteps was my sister who married her husband Harold soon after.

On weekends, my family and I would always get together for Sunday dinner and during the summers, we had backyard picnics. Everyone would bring their instruments and it would turn into a hoot-a-nanny (we weren't hillbillies but we just acted that way). I grew up in Croton, NY and it was the place where my story truly begins. What can I say about the town I grew up in...actually quite a bit. I was actually born in "The Old Ossining Hospital" on Spring Street in Ossining, NY (which is the next town over from Croton). The hospital is no longer there but most of us whose families lived in Croton were either born here or in The Old Peekskill Hospital. Now, for a little trivia: "The Old Ossining Hospital" was right next door to the Warden's House and the famous "Sing-Sing" prison. People mostly hear of Sing-Sing prison in many movies and it is located on the beautiful Hudson River and was also known as the town of Sing-Sing many years ago.

My father, Ellsworth Imm, was also born in Ossining in 1911 at home to his mostly German parents on the corner of Spring and Revolutionary Road (near the famous "Pine Tree Restaurant"). At about 5 years old, my father moved to the Archville section of Mt Pleasant Scarborough/Briarcliff/Tarrytown (which is now known as Sleepy Hollow, the town known for the "Headless Horsemen" famous legend). My dad's parents were mostly German and his mother came to Croton-on-Hudson from Germany as a little girl and grew up in the Mt. Airy section of the upper village. Her name was Mary Vespermann (my paternal grandmother) and she went to school on Grand Street in Croton in a little schoolhouse back in the late 1800's which is now "The Grand Street Firehouse". She later met my grandfather, Carl Imm, when she was the cook and he was the caretaker for John D. Rockefeller and his family in the town of Mt. Pleasant. My grandfather, Carl Imm came to this country from Europe (after being born in Poland to a German mother and a Russian father) and as an adult he lived in New York City for a short time and then settled in the Tarrytowns with his wife and they remained there until their deaths in 1963 and 1969. At twenty-five years old, my dad, Ellsworth Imm met my mother (another Croton girl). My mother Sarah Emery was born at home in a place referred to as "Soap Hill", which was off of Riverside Avenue in Croton in 1918. My father and my mother met in 1936 while she and her best friend Dot Kimball worked as waitresses at Julian's in Crotonville, NY. At a later point in 1936, my parents married and moved to Croton as a couple and lived there until their deaths in 1993 and 1994. My mother's friend Dot married my dad's brother Carl and they lived in Ossining. My Aunt Dot came from the Kimball family from Croton and was 1 of 9 children. Some of her family worked at The Van Cortlandt Manor House also located in Croton. In my mother's family, her mother, Margaret Place Emery was from Dutchess County. She was a Shecomeko Indian and my grandfather Nat Emery was from Elizabeth, New Jersey and his heritage derived from his family coming from Surrey England.. They married in the town in Dutchess County where former Croton-Harmon High School principal and Mayor of Croton Stanely H Kellerhouse, was from and lived in Croton until their deaths in 1956 and 1976. My mother's father worked as a pipefitter for New York Central plus he had his own side business and also worked for Mamie White

Funeral Home on Grand Street (which later became Carter's Funeral Home) which later moved to its new location where it stands today. My mother, Sarah Emery Imm, went to school in Croton at the Municipal Building and later at Croton-Harmon High School. Now, the Municipal Building named for Stanley H Kellerhouse is home to the Croton Police and village office workers as well as "The Croton Historical Society". Her parents lived in a few different places in Croton before building their permanent home on Hamilton Avenue near Van Wyck and Grand Street, a few houses in from the current funeral home and from the towns bed and breakfast. My brothers and sisters, Ellsworth (Ellie), Patty, Bobby, Mary and Lee also attended school in Croton and graduated from C.H.H.S as well. My children went to Croton schools at some points in their lives as well.

When I was little, until almost 3 years old, we lived across from where the "Tavern at Croton Landing" is now, which is formerly known as "Honeys". Honey's was the major spot to go for most Crotonite's and at one point Jackie Gleason star of the Honeymooners played pool there and even though now it is under new ownership, it still seems to be the hot spot in town. We lived at 4 Depot Square in front of the Old Croton North Station and Winklers along with many of the older original Croton families. Some names I remember are the Depalmas (my sister Mary's Godmother was Angie), Gibson's (my Godmother was Rose), Mezger's (my best friend Judie's family), Waters (Harold and Bobby owned Honeys for years), and D'Alvia's (Josephine was a historian in Croton for many years and her sons were attorneys and her husband Carl was the town judge). In this section of Croton, you had Brook Street, Farrington, Bank Street, and of course Riverside Avenue (which was also known as the Old Albany Post Road). A lot of people had to move because the "New 9" which we called it, was coming through so in order to build the highway, they started knocking down our homes to make room for the road. So we, "The Dock Rats", as we were referred to back then (from this section of Croton), had to find new homes.

In 1956, my parents bought a home in the Harmon section of Croton. We lived at 44 Oneida Avenue, 2 houses in from the Croton Carvel (where everyone seemed to gather socially).

CROTON CARVEL IN THE 1950'S CORNER
OF ONEIDA AND RIVERSIDE

When we moved into where the new homes stood, there were sand lots across the street and down on the corner of Oneida and Riverside. As kids, we used to play baseball and other sports in these sandlots. This section of Croton was named for Clifton Harmon who had a horse racetrack there before most of these homes were built on the street where I lived and it had been built with streets forming circles for the races. Near our home, some of the streets were Young Avenue, Hastings Avenue, Penfield Avenue, and Whelan and all of these connected to Benedict Boulevard and Cleveland Drive. We were also the children of many of the railroad workers. My dad, both of my grandfathers, some uncles, and 2 of my brothers worked there until their retirement or until they moved on to another phase in their life. I later married into a family where many of them also worked for the railroad. My husband's family was well-known in the workforce in Croton as they are the Anesi family. In the late 1800's early 1900's, they owned a tavern at the bottom of Mt. Airy Road and also across the street the stone house on Grand Street known as "The Gingerbread House", which was built by the Anesi family. The older generations of the Anesi's were stone masons that not only helped to build Croton Dam but many of the stone houses in Croton that have stood all of these years with such beauty and precision. My husband's grandfather, Marcus Anesi (whom my youngest son was named after), owned the stone house on Grand Street across from the foot of Mt. Airy. The family legend says that as the Anesi's were building this home, they wiped each stone by hand as the stones were put together. Also, the stone used in this home was said to have been leftover from the building of "The Croton Dam".

Well, now that I gave you some of my family history, I have to say growing up in Croton back in the '50s-'70's gave me a sense of security. When I was a child, I remember playing a lot of hopscotch in front of our house or jumping rope or hula-hooping. I never had to worry about being hurt like in these days when us as parents and grandparents worry about our kids being abducted or something worse. At a young age, we Croton kids had the Starlight Bowling Lanes, Miniature Golf, and the Drive-Inn. Our parents were never afraid of us walking there day or night or being hurt because it was a different age back then. Families back then knew each other by name and had each other's backs at all times. They were the good old days for sure. One last thing about growing up in Croton, it was also the home to many famous people such as Jackie Gleason (from The Honeymooners), Allen Funt and sons John who was in my class at C.E.T. and Peter Funt who took over the show after his father (Candid Camera), Gloria Swanson (actress). My mom would actually sleigh ride on Gloria Swanson's driveway as a child. Other famous people living in Croton were Peter Strauss (Rich Man/Poor Man series), Kathleen Beller (Dynasty), Greg Wangler (Folgers commercial and General Hospital), *and New Yorker Magazine's* artist Abe Birnbaum (whose wife, Frieda who was taken care of by me when I had my homecare business) who shared so many wonderful stories of their travels, Robert Klein (a famous comedian) whose parents had a house on Mt Airy and whose ex-wife Brenda Boozer (Metropolitan Opera Star) attended my church St. Mary's in Scarborough and sang in our choir when they lived in Briarcliff, and Peter Frampton (famous recording artist) who lived behind me on the outskirts of Croton in the '80's and many more which made Croton one DAM town for sure!

When I was 9 years old, I became very ill and spent months in the hospital diagnosed with a rare form of encephalitis. Years later, I would find out that it was actually Multiple Sclerosis. After being so ill as a child and the added exposure of other sick kids in the hospital ward (back then the kids were put into wards instead of private hospital rooms), I learned a lot about myself and my strength. We all had something different in the ward from Polio to Cystic Fibrosis, etc.

Seven months later, still being 9 years old, I came home from the hospital in Grasslands and from a Convalescent Home for Children, which was located in Chappaqua. Now, I seemed to look at life differently. I learned that prayers work. I became a nurturer to my family and friends while at the same time developing a strange psychic ability. It wasn't always that I was predicting the future but I would get feelings right before something was about to happen. Also, being sick for so long and away from the other kids at school caused some of them to bully and tease me when I returned because they heard I had a brain disease and assumed I was crazy. At the time, I had started experiencing panic attacks and even though I had a brain disease (which was thought to be Encephalitis), I later learned it was the beginning of M.S.

Chapter 2

TEENAGER FROM HELL

AFTER MY ILLNESS AS A child, as my parents would call it, I transitioned through what they called "the teen from hell" years. I was the rebel of rebels, I thought I had all of the answers, and I made my own rules. Though I never did drugs, I hung out with all different types of people (the greasers, the druggies, the losers, and even some nerds). I started smoking at thirteen, began drinking at sixteen, and became a clown. Even today, I have the ability to make people laugh at the most inappropriate times. As a teen, I had several boyfriends, some who were just friends over the years in the surrounding towns. At this point, I never took life too seriously.

One of the guys I had met when I was only twelve years old was named Johnny and he was in and out of my life until his untimely death (which was a month to the day of my eighteenth birthday). Johnny was not only my best friend, but he was also my boyfriend. I had just graduated from high school in June of 1971 and on August

7th, I came home from my job at the local Grand Union deli to find my parents and friends all waiting in my front yard waiting to tell me that Johnny had shot himself and died that day. Needless to say, I was overwhelmed by grief. I felt as though my own world had ended that day. Among some other horrors that summer, I had decided that it was time for me to settle down and grow up. On the night of my eighteenth birthday, my brother Lee's friend, Jack was at my house and his older brother came to pick him up after my birthday party. His brother, Don and I started talking and fourteen months later, Don became my husband. Don and I had lived two blocks apart and our fathers worked together. I assumed that it was fate that we should marry. After living through the events of that horrible summer before, I thought I was supposed to now live the American Dream. This would include the prince, the white picket fence, 2.5 kids, and to live happily ever after...Not!

MY WEDDING DAY NOVEMBER 4, 1972

Chapter 3

THE FAIRYTALE LIFE

DON AND I MARRIED IN November of 1972 and we had our first child, a perfect baby girl named Meg, in September of 1973. Six days after she was born, I turned twenty years old and was looking forward to a perfect life of watching my beautiful daughter accomplish all of the wonderful things she dreamed of. A year and a half later, my son Donnie was born and although I had a very difficult delivery, I was now told at twenty-one that I shouldn't have any more children because I had developed a rare form of toxemia which landed me on the critical list. I was happy having my boy and girl but growing up as one of six kids, I really wanted to have a large family.

Even though I was a new young mom, when Meg was a few months old, I had a feeling that something was terribly wrong with her. I couldn't put my finger on it but I still knew that something wasn't right. I spoke to her pediatrician and was assured that I was just being an anxious new mom and that it was probably just allergies. After a few years of caring for two babies, I started to notice that Meg seemed to cough a lot. When I kissed her, she tasted very salty and she had a very odd odor to her bowel movements. Though no one's B.M.'s smell great, there was an un-godly odor to hers. My son, Don, who was also in diapers, never emitted that kind of an odor.

I picked up one of Dr. Spock's baby books and although I had some medical background, I immediately turned to the page about the genetic illness called "Cystic Fibrosis". Most doctors in the '70's didn't even know much about this illness. I called her doctor right away and asked for her to be sweat tested (this is how they tested for C.F.). After much resistance, her doctor agreed to schedule the test but she acted as if I were being a "Drama Queen".

We went to the County Medical Center where they performed the sweat test and it resulted in being positive for Cystic Fibrosis. We immediately left Westchester County Medical Center and went directly to the pediatrician's office. She looked at us and basically said how sorry she was. My perfect little girl would probably die between her 5th and 10th birthday. At this point, she was five months shy of her 3rd birthday. Because C.F. was a genetic illness meant that both my husband and I had carried the gene and in each child we had together, there would be a 1 in 4 chance that they would also inherit this dreadful illness. Our son was just 1 ½ years old at the time and he now needed to be tested also. After trying to deal with this nightmare diagnosis, we were now going to see if our son was going to face the same fate as our precious little girl.

It was the week before Easter and we took our oldest son, Donnie for the sweat test and we were told his test result was on the borderline and that he possibly had C.F. too. The doctors told us that he should be tested again in a couple of weeks to be sure. We went home to try to comprehend all of this and to wait it out again until our son's next test.

It was now the Friday before Easter (Good Friday) and my dad worked for our church and being brought up a devout Christian, I believed that God wouldn't give us any more than we could handle. My husband and I were very numb and Easter was not looking too much like a new beginning,

Ironically, the house across the street from where we lived belonged to a family friend of mine whom I had grown up with and their niece had just come to visit. I hadn't seen their niece since high school and while I was outside on this Good Friday getting some fresh air, the niece saw me and not knowing what we were going through said she had recently become "born again" and felt that for some reason she had needed to go to her uncles' house that day. We began to chat and I told her what I was going through with my children. Although Meg's test was positive and Donnie's test was leaning towards positive, she asked me if she could pray with the kids and at that point I figured it couldn't hurt.

MEG AND DONNIE EASTER 1976

Chapter 4

Easter Miracle

Shortly after Easter, we went back to have my son retested and this time the test was negative. I truly believe that we had an Easter miracle and this was the beginning of many unexplained events that would take place throughout my life.

Although Meg did have C.F. when we went back to Westchester Medical Center, at that time, the doctor who headed the C.F. Center, Dr. Armond Mascia (our personal angel) was one of the kindest human beings I have ever known. He told us that our daughter was the healthiest looking child with C.F. he had ever seen and to keep doing whatever I was doing before she was diagnosed (in addition to supplementing her with some vitamins, enzymes, and chest physical therapy). Because she had C.F., Meg needed to consume 3 times the amount of food that a normal child would have eaten which was due to the fact of the pancreatic insufficiency of breaking down the fats and malabsorption. The doctor had also prescribed salt pills for dehydration as children with CF lost salt more than other people when they would sweat.

For the next six years, Meg did very well and right before her 10th birthday she started to have some stomach issues due to the C.F. (though none of the lung issues ever manifested at this time which usually killed people with C.F.). After the gastro problems were under control, she stayed symptom-free of any lung issues for many years. It was many months of trying to get her digestive problems under control which included the use of stool softeners, drinking mineral oil, senekot laxatives, and also having to drink Mucomyst (which we referred to as "rotten eggs"). It was some kind of a sulfa drug that broke down the thick mucus that would clog the intestines of C.F. kids. It was not a fun time but she got through it. Despite the fact that she was only 9 years old at the time, she defied the odds and took it like a trooper.

Chapter 5

My Born Again Years

After Meg's diagnosis, I became very involved in the Cystic Fibrosis Foundation by raising the publics' awareness and increasing fund-raising events to benefit the research of Cystic Fibrosis. Meg also got very involved and she became the poster child for C.F. and assisted in our fund-raising efforts. I thank my father-in-law for what he told me after her initial diagnosis which is what motivated me to let the world know that we were going to fight this disease all the way. He said, *"You can either do nothing and feel sorry for yourselves or you can go out and let the world know you're going to do something constructive"*.

During this time, I also got deeper into the meaning of life and God and did not blame him for what happened to us. I prayed a lot and things went well for many years, with just some minor setbacks. Meg remained fairly healthy and in 1981 I found myself pregnant again. I was being told how Cystic Fibrosis could happen again and of course due to my own health issues during my second pregnancy (in which I almost died); I had to make a decision. I went full-term and had my third child, Danny who was tested for C.F. and was disease-free. Life was finally looking up!

Being born again, you are taught to not read horoscopes or to listen to psychics along with many other forbidden things. So by trying to follow these beliefs, I distanced myself from people who would get into this kind of stuff. Even though I knew I had been given somewhat of a gift myself, I still went into some type of denial about my own abilities.

Right before Christmas, my best friend then Denise (friends since the age of 2), called and said for my Christmas present she was going to a psychic party and had paid for me to go with her. I hesitated but then I let my guard down and against my better judgment, I decided to go. There were about twenty women whom I had never met before and they knew nothing about me. When it was time for my reading, the psychic blew my mind with her findings. Along with many things she had told me, she was correct in recalling my concerns about my aging parents (my mother was just starting to exhibit signs of dementia which wound up being Alzheimer's disease and my father was diagnosed with C.O.P.D). She also said that my 3 children would be fine which gave me hope that my daughter would live a normal life, not knowing at the time that 7 years later I would have a fourth child. She also told me I was a special child of God and I assumed at the time it was my work I had been doing for the Cystic Fibrosis Foundation. I replied to her, "We are all special children of God". She said, "No, you have a special gift that you need to bring to the world". Out of all of the twenty women, she stated that she would like to see me again and that I was chosen to make a difference in this world. Now, twenty-five years later, I've realized that I need to tell my story and that's precisely what she had meant. I believe we should all take our negative experiences and turn them into positive ones. Like the Chinese ying and yang symbolizes, I believe that is what the balance in the world truly is. Don't get me wrong, I have been depressed and have felt like giving up, but then I seem to find something that makes me go on. I thank our Creator for the strength.

Chapter 6

THE END OF AN ERA

N ow, we are in the mid '80's: my daughter was now in her teens and not doing badly at all with the exception of some setbacks. She was becoming more independent. In 1986, we were asked to be guests on *The Live with Regis and Kathie Lee Morning Show* on channel 7 in which we talked about our experiences with Cystic Fibrosis. Meg and I were both nervous but we went to NYC and appeared on the show and continued our fund-raising events. At fifteen years old, Meg became a co-recipient of the Charles Lubin Humanitarian Award for her work with C.F. In 1988, I found myself pregnant again and I gave birth in November to my 4th child Marc. Although he was born full-term and weighted 9 lbs. 9 ozs, I found out that he also had Cystic Fibrosis. He appeared to be physically perfect in every way with the exception of his disease. Even though we knew it could happen again, we dealt with it the best way we could. Meg was now going on sixteen and was not only a sister to this beautiful little boy but also a second mother. They also shared the bond of having Cystic Fibrosis. When Marc was diagnosed with C.F. at 5 days old, Meg had turned to me and said, *"Mom, you got me thru this and now we will get him through this together"*.

Now, being a teen, she like all girls her age, had raging hormones which started kicking in and she became the rebel. She started dating and was still pretty healthy except for a sinus surgery. My little girl was becoming a woman. She was now driving me crazy by doing what she wanted and by living life to the fullest and then some. Things were getting tough and even though she knew she had a lung disease, I found out she tried to smoke cigarettes and then experimented with pot. But, we got through this stage. Beginning with some lung involvement, she casted her cares to the wind and her slogan was "No Fear". At seventeen, she moved in with her boyfriend and at the age of twenty-one, she gave birth to her son, Christopher. Three years later, she had a daughter named Amber. During Amber's birth, Meg's lung collapsed. She became a terrific mom and even though her health started diminishing, she fought it all the way. She worked as a waitress, babysat, etc. About two years after her daughter's birth, both lungs started deteriorating. For the last seven months of her life, she was in and out of the hospital. She came home at the end of April in 2002 and we were hoping to get her on the double lung transplant list but on May 12, 2002 (Mother's Day), while she was at home surrounded by her kids, she lost the battle that she had fought so hard. At this time, Chris was 7 years old and Amber was 4. Meg was almost twenty-nine years old when she passed away and she defied many odds but in those twenty-nine years, she touched many and made a big difference in all of our lives. She was not only an inspiration to people and young adults battling Cystic Fibrosis but to mothers in general. She was a wonderful mom and even taught me to be a better mother. I truly believe the Lord chose Mother's Day to take her home with him because of the "special mother" she was and she would not be forgotten. She touched so many lives.

MY LATE SON MARC WITH MY
GRANDCHILDREN AMBER AND CHRIS

(MEG'S CHILDREN)

Chapter 7

LIFE CHANGES

M<small>ANY CHANGES HAVE OCCURRED SINCE</small> the 1990's. Our family lost so many of our loved ones. I sometimes look at our family pictures and it kind of reminds me of the movie "Back to the Future" when Michael J. Fox is on stage and is holding his family pictures and everyone starts disappearing one by one.

We all have had losses as life is a waiting game. We lose grandparents, aunts, uncles, etc. From my own history, my eldest sisters' husband had died in 1991, my dad died in 1993, my mom died in 1994, my brother died in 1998, my daughter died in 2002, and in May of 2006, I lost my sister who was my support. Also between these deaths, I had lost all of my uncles and aunts along with some of my friends.

This is why I am now dedicated to writing this book. Not only is it about our lives but what has happened since their deaths. Though at times I lost it and started to act like an idiot, I began drinking too much and went into a state of denial but now I have decided that it was time to make some changes in my life.

Chapter 8

THE NEXT 50 YEARS

Now that I have covered the first fifty years of my story, we will get down to what this book is truly about. Since my daughter's death on Mother's Day of 2002, a lot of strange things have happened and they are described within the title of my book.

I guess I should it began on the very day she passed. I was living by myself while sharing custody of my sons with my husband so the kids were with their father that weekend. I had planned to go to see my daughter that day. But, my car had broken down and I was waiting for someone to bring me to her house. I kept calling her and ended up getting the answering machine instead. Everyone was busy because it was Mother's Day so I assumed that I just had to wait for my sister's kids to leave so she could pick me up. I decided to cook something at home to bring to Meg before I left. All of a sudden, my dog started to howl, something that I had never heard him do before. Finally, I received a call from my estranged husband and he said that something had happened to my daughter but he wasn't sure what was going on. At this point, I got a weird feeling and I called my sister who came and got me right away. I was told they took my daughter to the hospital. Not knowing which hospital she was admitted to, I assumed it was the Community Hospital about a mile away from where she lived. My sister arrived and when we got to the hospital, I saw my family members gathered outside. As we approached the Emergency Room, I was greeted by the Chaplin and was informed that the doctors did everything they possibly could but she didn't make it. She initially died at home and they couldn't revive her after countless efforts at the hospital. The family went in to say their goodbyes and we left and went back to my estranged husband's house.

Friends and family all gathered around us at my estranged husband's house on that Mother's Day. A lot of my daughter's friends came over to be with us and had remarked about the rare formation of the moon and stars that night which were the exact formation of my daughter's tattoo on her back. Knowing that I wasn't into her getting tattoos, I never paid too much attention until that evening. Later on, I would find out that another one of her tattoos would spark my interest.

Everyone left and my other kids went to bed. I couldn't sleep so I called my younger brother, Lee, who always had a way of putting my mind at ease. During the course of the conversation, I remarked that I wished Meg would give me a sign when all of a sudden the stereo came on while flashing lights and the cd changer began turning and the player was repeatedly opening and shutting itself. At that point, I screamed and woke up my entire house. Needless to say, it freaked me out.

Chapter 9

More Signs

I FINALLY FELL ASLEEP FOR A couple of hours all the while knowing how tough the next couple of days would be. When I woke up, I went outside on the patio to collect my thoughts. When the phone rang the next morning, it was my daughter's best friend Christine. My son brought the phone outside to me when I noticed a butterfly that kept flying near me. At first, I didn't think much of it but it just stayed with me the whole time while I was talking to her friend. I told her how this butterfly was acting and she told me that my daughter's third and final tattoo was a butterfly on her ankle. Meg always wore socks around me so I didn't even know she had it. Then, her friend told me how Meg loved butterflies. This was something my daughter never told me.

When the call-waiting beeped on my phone, it was one of my other friends so I told Christine to hold on and then the butterfly flew away. Ironically, my daughter's friend and my friend lived across the street from one another. As I hung up on my friend in order to switch back to Christine, the butterfly came back and sat right beside me. I told Christine to come over and see the butterfly. When she arrived, the butterfly flew to her, circled her car, and when she sat down with me, it followed her and sat down between our chairs. Now, to put it to the test, I asked God if this was a sign from my daughter and if so for God to let the butterfly walk under the chair where her friend was sitting and that was exactly what it did. I couldn't believe it! In less than twenty-four hours since my daughter's passing, this was now the third sign I had witnessed.

A few hours later, my youngest son who was thirteen, was pretty irrational and acting out. He began yelling at his dad and just as he walked out the door, the wind blew an empty twelve pack box of Pepsi and it hit him in the arm. All I could think of is my daughter's love of Pepsi (she never went anywhere without a bottle of Pepsi). It was as if she were letting him know that she was watching him and to shape up. We never found out where that Pepsi box even came from. After I made the funeral arrangements, I was sitting alone and decided to write a poem about her. I named it "My Special Angel".

My brother's daughter, Melissa called and told me what happened to her the day after Meg died. My daughter used to babysit Melissa when she was young. It was the end of the school year and Melissa was taking a final exam. When she got to school she found it very hard to concentrate since she had lost her cousin, Meg, the day before the exam took place. When Melissa entered the classroom right before the exam, she chose a desk she had never sat at before and when she looked down at the wooden desk, she saw the words "Meg was here" with a heart around it. She couldn't believe this as that was my daughter's name. She ran out of the classroom and began crying.

Chapter 10

One Last Hug

Though life would never be the same again, I was in the next stage of a mother's grief. I needed to start living again and to go back to work. Still, without my car (as the engine was blown), I needed to get some supplies from the store. So my friend Kathy Herde said that since her kids were off from school that day that she would pick me up so we could go shopping and out to lunch. When Kathy showed up with her younger daughter and her daughter's friend, I didn't really pay attention to the girls. When we went to the Wendy's restaurant, I noticed that her daughter's friend bore a striking resemblance to my own daughter when she was younger. Just like my daughter, she had green eyes and freckles on her nose. Of course, this little girl knew nothing about me or my recent loss.

We went into Wendy's to get some food and as we got to our table, this little girl threw her arms around me and began to weep. It was as if she were in a trance. A few seconds later, she looked at me and asked what just happened and she couldn't figure out why she had been hugging me and crying. Ironically, earlier that morning I had been on the phone with another one of my friends and she had asked me if I could have anything in the world what would I ask for? I replied, "One last hug from my daughter". I guess my daughter came through again. The strange thing was that Kathy didn't even know that I talked to the friend that morning and how I had made the statement to her about "the last hug".

Chapter 11

My Special Angel

I FINALLY MOTIVATED MYSELF TO RETURN to work. Since I had taken so much time off during my daughter's illness, I was forced to drive a taxi. At this point, I had lost my apartment and had to stay at my estranged husband's until I could get back on my feet.

Since my daughter's death occurred at her home, I couldn't even drive by her house because it was too painful. Then, one night while I was driving the cab, my route was on her street and as I passed by her house, a song came on the oldies station called, "My Special Angel". If you remember in the beginning of my book, the title of this song was also the name of the poem I wrote for her. Chills went through my body along with a sense of peace.

After a few weeks went by, the same song came on again just as I passed by her house. It was just too much of a coincidence for me. The third time that it had happened, a friend of mine named April was with me (she lived a few blocks from where my daughter had lived). When I brought April home, I passed by Meg's house and told April what had happened the previous 2 times I drove past my daughter's street. April's face had a look of disbelief because just as we had passed by my daughters' house, the song played again and we were so shaken up that we both started crying and we pulled off onto the side of the road. I couldn't drive anymore because I was shaking so badly. I guess my daughter was just letting me know that she was my "special angel" after all. A few months before Meg's death, ironically, April had brought me a little porcelain angel as a gift because she said she felt she needed to give it to me.

Chapter 12

As Time Goes By

AS THE YEARS HAVE GONE by, other signs began to manifest. Things began to happen to other members of the family and friends. I had shared my strange experiences with those closest to me.

My granddaughter was planting a garden with her paternal grandmother as a memorial to her mother (my daughter). While putting the flowers in the ground at her grandmothers' house, butterflies started to surround them. I assumed it was another way of my daughter letting us know that she was still with us, as the butterfly seemed to be very significant ever since my daughter's death.

Not long after this, my sister Mary called me (who lives 40 miles away from me), and she told me something that had happened to her and also related to butterflies. Mary suffers from long term Lyme disease and Fibromyalgia and she had to get her blood work done on this particular morning. On her way to the lab, she arrived and found out that the lab was closed. She went to another lab and it was also closed. At this point, she was hungry and felt weak because she had been fasting due to the lab work she needed to have done. She ended up going to a deli she had never been to before and as she pulled into the deli's parking lot, butterflies started surrounding her. As she walked into the deli, she ran into my son-in-law's parents (my deceased daughter's in-laws). Another strange coincidence is that this deli was about fifteen miles from my sister's house and fifty from my son-in-law's parents, as they were on their way to Albany because they were taking their daughter to college. What are the odds of them meeting up at this deli which was technically out of the way for both of them? This is another sign I presume.

Chapter 13

MORE BUTTERFLIES TO COME

M Y OTHER SISTER PATTY WHO passed away in May of 2006 also had an unusual experience with a butterfly about a year or two before she passed away. Patty was a skeptic about life after death and when I told her some of the stories relating to different signs that my family was experiencing, she would laugh at me and call me a kook. Patty and I were very different even though we were sisters. She was very quiet and laid back and I was always very loud and outgoing. I would joke with her over the years at the fact that I must have gotten some extra hormones that she was lacking in.

Pat lived a very quiet life and she married at seventeen, had 3 kids, and when she turned 48 years old, her husband developed pancreatic cancer and died 6 weeks after his initial diagnosis. After his passing, she became very bitter about life. She had a severe panic disorder for years, didn't drive at the time, and hardly ever left her house due to her disorder. She really was quite dependent on her husband so after he passed away, she had to do everything by herself. She finally overcame her panic disorder after getting on the right medication and she learned to drive.

To get back to her butterfly episode, she was out in her yard one day trimming her hedges since she owned 1 ½ acres of land. She heard her phone ringing but she was too far away to run towards the phone and at that moment, a huge monarch butterfly flew up to her and she got a strange feeling that it was me on the other end of the phone. She went into the house to receive her messages and though it could have been several people, it was me letting her know that I was rushing my youngest son, Marc (who was fifteen years old at the time) to the hospital as he suffered from Cystic Fibrosis also. This was the first time he had to be hospitalized because now he had been having lung issues due to this disease. From that day on, she became a believer of signs.

Though Marc survived his first lung exacerbation, a few weeks later, Pat was diagnosed with cancer (Non-Hodgkin's Lymphoma). She started chemotherapy soon after and though she had been told she had third stage lymphoma the doctors also found nodes in her stomach. After chemo, the doctors did a PET scan and said the nodes had shrunk and even though she was sixty-three years old, she could probably live another twenty years before she had any more problems. At the time, she said to me that she would most likely live until she was eighty. Unfortunately, she only lived another six months after her chemo ended due to her contracting ARDS (Acute Respiratory Distress Syndrome). As her family, we didn't know why she got this disease but we can only assume it was caused because of complications resulting from the chemo as she lived the life of a tee-totaler. She had never even drank or smoked during her entire life. She ended up dying on May 20th, 2006. Ironically, my daughter, my sister, and my mom all died in May, a week apart from each other as my daughter died on May 12 and my mom died on May 26. Though spring is a time of new beginnings, it's not always been a happy time for my family. Due to Meg's death 4 years prior to Pat's death (which was also in May), I also just got my son Marc out of the hospital after his second exacerbation of lung issues with his Cystic Fibrosis.

Chapter 14

RAINBOWS

ON THE DAY THAT PAT died, it was a bright spring day in the eyes of the world meaning the day itself was beautiful and sunny. My phone rang and it was my family telling me that my sister had passed away. I called her only daughter, Sue and I said I would come and help them make arrangements. I arrived at my sister's house and was greeted by her eldest son, Scott. My nephew, her son, and her daughter's husband, Wayne began to talk about what comes next. I tried to assure them that we would survive this too and because of my strong belief in the after-life, she was okay. As we started to talk about religion and God, I spoke to them about all of the signs I had seen after my daughter's death and hoped it would also put their mind at ease that life doesn't end here on earth. I started with a story about my father 6 months prior to his death on April 18, 1993 who also happened to be their grandfather. As I began to tell this story, I myself recognized the butterfly connection had actually started then.

My dad and I were sitting on his deck one day in October of 1992 (6 months prior to his death). My dad and I were very close and in many ways we were a lot alike. I was the youngest girl and the 5th of 6 kids. Like him, I am very strong-willed and at the time, he knew he didn't have much time left because he was on oxygen constantly as a result of his C.O.P.D. He was now eighty-one years old, had smoked for over sixty years, and he worked with asbestos. As a side job, he worked for our church and he was very religious for all of his life. Because of his strong belief in religion, he started to wonder what death would be like. I turned to him as words came from my mouth like I were listening to someone else speak. I said, "While on earth, I think our bodies are like the caterpillar and death to me was the release of the butterfly with all of the beauty that surrounds it". All of a sudden, I saw such peace in his face and then he and I changed the subject.

After telling my sisters' children this story and as we listened to my sister's favorite music, the phone began to ring. My niece went to answer it and as she was talking I continued to tell stories of other signs that I believed were from beyond this realm and all of a sudden, as she stood by the sliding glass doors overlooking my sisters' deck, there appeared a double rainbow. It seemed to be meant just for us. Now, at fifty-four years old, I can honestly say I had never experienced a rainbow so beautiful in my life. I grabbed my camera phone and took a picture. As of that day of my sister's death, her kids had now become believers in the signs.

Chapter 15

RADIO CONNECTION

ON THE DAY OF MY sister's funeral, all of my family had gathered after the burial and we went to a hall to sit down to eat. During the conversation with my brother, nieces, and nephews, somehow the topic came up of more strange occurrences. My brother, Bob said that on the day that our sister died, he went out to his wife's car and all of a sudden the radio came on by itself. The strange part was that the key had not been turned on for the radio to even work. My niece Sue had said while she was at work that morning, the volume on the radio at the bank where she worked started to go up and down as if someone had been playing with it. That same morning, as I was putting on my face in the mirror, I got the news of my sister's passing. I then turned on the radio and all of a sudden it started making strange noises and the sound was going in and out and at that time, I had not realized what was going on. It was only after speaking to the rest of my family as we put our radio stories together that we had finally realized it had happened to all three of us at about the same time of my sister's passing.

If you can recall, on the night that my daughter died, when I asked for a sign, the radio started going berserk. They say that this is one of the ways our departed come through to us to let us know they are still around due to the fact that they say we are all made up of energy.

Chapter 16

THE PHONE RINGS

A FEW WEEKS AFTER MY SISTER'S death, I had been on the phone with my other sister Mary. She went into a story about how she had gone to bed the night before and she had not been feeling well so she shut the ringer off on her phone. In the early morning, she heard her phone ringing (and the ringer was still in the "off" position). As she put the phone up to her ear, she heard a voice repeatedly saying "Hello Mary" and again "Hello Mary". There was no doubt in her mind that the voice belonged to our newly deceased sister, Patty. To this day, Mary is bewildered as to how this all happened.

After listening to her story and trying to make sense of what she had told me, we ended our conversation. I decided to call my brother Bob and then he tells me something that had happened to him on that same morning. As he went down into the laundry room to get the clothes from the dryer, he heard a voice saying his name. He was the only one at home and as he looked around he realized it was the voice of our recently departed sister. He told me how frightened he was and he went upstairs to his living room in order to relax. A year before this, he had to retire due to a heart attack and seizures. I was very concerned about him because of his own health issues and I tried to keep him calm. I told him that I had spoken to Mary that morning and what she had told me about the phone call she received. Bob had not talked to Mary and he had no idea of the eerie call she had received that morning.

I know this may sound crazy and unbelievable to most, but I myself don't understand how these things can happen. I guess there are things we just can't explain during this lifetime. Like I have previously said in other chapters, I too have had many things happen to me that I can't explain but as time goes by, I guess that's the reason I found the need within myself to write about them.

I recently had my own experience with the telephone that I can't explain. During the week of mine and my daughter's birthday in September of 2007, my daughter would have turned thirty-four on September 1, 2007 and I turned fifty-four on September 7th. It seems the loss of our family around the times of birthdays and holidays are the toughest. I try to go through these times the best I can but I think about the people I have lost and what life would be like if they were still with us.

During September 12th, 2007 I received a strange phone call. The previous day was the 6 year anniversary of 9/11, a day in which I was thinking of my former co-worker, Carol B. who had lost her son Michael on 9/11/01. This date was four days after my birthday and ten after my daughter's birthday. September 11th is also the birthdays of my sister Mary's two daughters, Holly and Wendi.

After watching all of the reminders of what happened on September 11th and by thinking back on these past 6 years to when my daughter was still alive, at that point, I remembered how frightened she was on that horrific day. She was still at home but was really worried about the lives of everyone and what would happen because of the terrorists' plots on our country. She really worried about everyone else even though she was so ill herself.

After thinking about her and 9/11, my phone began to ring and no one was speaking on the other end. But, as I looked at my caller I.D., it said "caller unknown" but for whatever reason the numbers made sense to me. If you broke the numbers down it was the day, month, and year of my daughter's birthday and above where it said "unknown" on the phone, the bottom numbers were 9-1-1. Ironically, my TV was on at the same time and the Montel Williams show was on and the famous Sylvia Brown was the guest and the first thing she spoke of was mysterious phone calls from beyond. I truly believe this was another message meant for me. As the call came from my home phone, I grabbed my cell phone and took a picture of the call.

Lately, I have been on the internet and have noticed that I was having similar experiences to other people who have lost their children. I've also been reading books on life after death. One in particular that caught my interest was written by a minister named Don Piper. The name of his book is "90 Minutes in Heaven". The book is about his own personal experiences with life after death. I strongly recommend it for all of those who are looking for answers whether they want to face it or not. We will all have losses and I believe that books like this will make life a little easier for you.

Chapter 17

WHY ME?

WHEN WE LOSE PEOPLE THAT we are close to or we ourselves get sick, I don't care what walk of life you come from whether it be blue-collar, white-collar, homeless, entrepreneur, etc. In the end, we will all share the same fate. Though we try not to think about it, it is reality.

After my losses, I've found out who my true friends are. Especially after my daughters' death, I saw a lot of people who I thought were friends walk away from me. At times, I felt like I was the one that had died! In many ways, the person I once was died but I like to think I kind of went through my own process of metamorphosis. I've changed in many ways but as I write this book, I realize the changes I have made in my life are for the better. Though I am far from perfect, but then again, who is?

I have always been the one people would call when they had problems and I would try to help people put things into the proper perspective. Even as a young adult before my losses, I had suffered over the years but I always tried to help people. Like I said, I am not perfect. There were years I drank too much and I acted like a fool doing things I look back on and if I hadn't been under the influence, I never would have thought of doing such things.

After my estranged husband and I split in 1994, we remained living under the same roof for a while because we couldn't afford to live apart at the time. But, we eventually went on to be our own people. When I started dating again, it was after my marriage which consisted of twenty-three with my husband since I was eighteen years old right up until my forty-first birthday. First, I would like to say we grew apart and were no longer compatible and it had nothing to do with finding someone else. Several months went by before I even thought about dating again. I had a few serious relationships afterwards, but I soon found out that I was looking for love in all the wrong places and acting out in anger of all the hurt life had shown me.

Chapter 18

Love Yourself First

After my menopausal breakdown (as I like to refer to it) and after I made some bad decisions in love and life, I finally took some time to learn to love me. Even through all of my losses, and all of my stupid mistakes, I found it could be done.

I am now fifty-four and I feel like it has finally happened. Though I not only lost people I loved dearly, I lost my house to foreclosure in July 2001 and then in May 2002, after my daughter's death, I lost my apartment. I've worked many years with the elderly while doing my own homecare business. But, in November of 1992, I was in a very serious automobile accident and was laid up for a couple of years eventually to find out that I had Multiple Sclerosis. I was told that because of my head injury in the auto accident, it brought out the disease in its totality. Even though I believe I have suffered from M.S. since I was nine years old. I could no longer care for the elderly and instead tried my hand at a few different professions including going back to school in 1999 and passing the NYS state test to become a P&C insurance agent. Then, my daughter was getting sick on and off and I would take time off of work to help her. It got to the point where I couldn't keep a job for very long not only because of her illness but also because my M.S. was starting to take a toll on me. Walking can be difficult at times and I tire easily but hide it well. A lot of people think I am still the high energy person that I've been known for most of my life not realizing over the past few years there were days I struggled to get out of bed.

I will talk more about the M.S. and caring for my other child in the next chapters, but if I did not learn to love myself, I probably would have given up by now. I learned that just because I have been limited by caring for my two children with Cystic Fibrosis and now limited myself mostly because of the M.S. that we all need to love the person inside (which is the soul), the core of our existence, because illness and death cannot destroy that. We shouldn't allow it to destroy who we really are.

Though I've asked after my daughters' death for "one last hug", I am now trying to embrace my own being so I can continue to help others. Knowing the kind of person she was, I know she would have wanted me to continue my fight.

Chapter 19

WHEN THE GOING GETS TOUGH, THE TOUGH GET GOING

D ON'T GET ME WRONG, THERE are times even now that I feel despondent but I know that that is a waste of energy. I can be writing the book even on my bad days when I am not feeling well because of the M.S. while I was helping to care for my son and his needs due to C.F. Everyday began with getting up and getting my son's meds ready and sterilizing his equipment for his nebulizer treatments. He took several pills throughout the day as well as up to five nebulizer treatments at least twice a day along with a pulmonary vest to clear his lungs and administering IV meds. Though I have limited energy a lot of the time, somehow we got through it together. He was a typical teenager who just happened to have a chronic illness. Though he was 18, he didn't seem to go past 96 lbs. He also suffered from liver disease from C.F. and related diabetes but he didn't let that stop him from living life to the fullest. He drove and worked on his car and recently had a part-time job. He had many friends and he was definitely his own person.

Though the prognosis for C.F. is not great, we tried to live life in the present and unwrap everyday as a gift because that is all any of us want whether we are sick or not. None of us are promised a tomorrow so we need to experience today in the best way that we can.

I know I have touched on birth, death, and everything in between but if I can give hope to one person and belief because of my own real life experiences and my familiar, from the known and the unknown, then I'll know I've contributed something to this wonderful experience we call life.

I am sure there will be some who read my book and like my sister thought before her own experience with the monarch butterfly, think I am a nut, but that's okay. I know what I have been through and what I have experienced. Since the beginning of time, many a skeptic was born and many I am sure will take this attitude to their own demise.

My own experiences have made me love life to the fullest and to open and expand my own mind and hopefully it will help others who are open to do so too! Many look for answers while others simply exist. You can't win everyone over or we would solve the problems of the world and all of the wars would end.

Chapter 20

Deborah Hanlon (The Medium)

Earlier in the dedications section of my book, I talked about a party I went to at my friend Carol Moran's house. Carol had been to a party at another friend's house prior to our get together with Deborah. Carol is an Awareness through Movement therapist and works with everything from autism to strokes, etc. Carol is also a very spiritual person. After meeting Deborah, for those who don't know what a medium is, they are people who can receive messages from the other side. Like I mentioned in my last chapter, if you are a skeptic then maybe you should go and see one and I am sure you will change your mind. After Carol saw Deborah, she decided to have her party and told me that she felt I was the reason she met Deborah in the first place. Carol was one of the people who supported me in the writing of my own book and even though I began writing the book before I met Deborah, she felt I should meet with her. I was the last to arrive at Carol's get together and before I arrived I was told Deborah spoke of three names: Margaret, Stephanie, and Ron. I thought to myself before my reading that Margaret is my daughter's formal name and also Stephanie is my daughter's stepdaughter's name. Also, I have 2 cousins paternal and maternal by the names of Ron who I seldom see.

I was the last of the 6 people to go in for my reading as I never had been to a medium before (though I have watched them on Montel Williams, read Sylvia Brown's books, as well as John Edwards books and show "Cross Country"). Twenty-five years ago, I did see a psychic who spoke only of the present but not of the dead.

As soon as I walked in, the medium named Deborah looked at me and said, "You have lost many including a child. She then went on to say, "Your daughter is here right now and wants me to give you a hug". She then told me that my daughter is proud of the way I am overseeing things for her kids which are my grandchildren, Chris and Amber. She also told me that when my granddaughter is older, she will also have a gift. During the session, the medium told me that my daughter wanted her (the medium) to hold my hands as we proceeded. The next person to come through was my eldest brother, Ellie who died on April 21, 1998 on the day before his sixty-first birthday. She told me that he is laughing at me which I later found out from my brother's wife meant that he thought I was funny. I have always had a sense of humor. Also, my sister-in-law said he thought I was hysterical. The next to come through was my sister and Deborah the medium mentioned two names that made no sense to me but finally as we put the names together it turned out to be the name of a little organ my dad bought me when I was 5 years old. One day as my sister Pat was cleaning, she wanted me to move so she could dust the table and the organ I was playing was sitting on the table. After a temper tantrum, I banged on the keys and one of them stuck so after that my sister stuck a match cover under the key so you couldn't tell the key was broken. She got me to do what I was told by singing what I call "*The Emenee Organ Song*". Because of this, I didn't think she would threaten to tell our dad about what I did. so I behaved for her. No one knew about this but my sister and I never even told my friends. She also said my sister mentioned the butterfly in her back yard.

The next one to come through was my Dad. First, Deborah said my dad mentioned his coffin and I immediately knew what she meant. The medium even thought that it was weird that my dad would come through and talk about his own coffin. Then I told her about the night of my dad's wake (Dad passed away on my sister's birthday on April 18, 1993). At the time, my 3 brothers were there and 2 sisters and myself and as we were talking about a ring that my father wanted that mom had bought for him that he was wearing in his coffin. My oldest brother said, "What should we do with this ring after the wake"? I said Dad waited forever to even get this ring made and there were 6 of us talking about it. I spoke up and then said, "He should be buried with it on". Just as I said this, I looked over at my dad in the coffin and all of a sudden his hands that were laid across his chest broke loose and went up in the air and then to his sides. I started hyperventilating and by the time of the next viewing, the undertaker had to fix his hands and to lay them on his chest as they were at the start of the wake. Deborah said my father's spirit, like most, was at his own wake and he heard what we were saying and made his hands do that. What were the chances of that happening?

The next thing that Deborah said was that my dad was calling me a nickname, "Pokey". I didn't remember until the day after my reading that my dad used to tell me that I was a slowpoke and at times when I was younger, he did refer to me as "Pokey". Deborah told me that my dad said to tell me that he stood by me in spirit and was holding me up on the day of my daughter's funeral at the church where he worked for fifty years. The next person to come through was my mom. Deborah said my mom was holding a caramel colored candy between her thumb and forefinger. At first, this didn't make any sense to me until I realized that mom used to suck on Halls' cough drops all the time and that's what they looked like. Last but not least, she said Angie came through and then I realized it was my boyfriend John who had died when I was seventeen's mother named Angie. She also told me that I should finish writing my book. So here I am...

On the way home from my reading, I got a ride with someone from the party who I didn't know all that well but was going my way. During our conversation, I found out that he was in a speech class with my cousin Ron. Before I got into the party with the medium, Ron was the third name that was mentioned. His name was mentioned even before I arrived along with Margaret (my daughter), Stephanie (my step-granddaughter), and Ron (my cousin).

Chapter 21

TV Mediums

I WOULD LIKE TO THANK THE mediums that have gone on TV and have made a difference in many lives including mine. They have given hope to so many through the media as an outlet. I am sure they know about all of the skeptics but as many of them know how the veil is thinning between this world and the next and hopefully more and more people will come to terms with the truth. I unfortunately had to go through a lot of losses to come to terms with this truth and had to be shown that there is a light at the end of the tunnel...literally! I don't get why people don't believe in life after death as many attend Church for the same reason so why the disbelief of what I am telling you?

I could have thanked you at the end of my book but I felt you all deserved a chapter to yourselves. Thanks again to Intuitive Medium Deborah and John Edwards. I love you both!

Chapter 22

M.S. And Me

I PROBABLY SHOULD HAVE SAID ME and M.S. as my chapter title. What people need to realize is that you are always you. M.S. doesn't define you, Cancer is not you, and Cystic Fibrosis is not you.

I hope that one day people will learn to define a person who has an illness as a person first and look at all of the wonderful qualities they have. Don't dwell directly on their illness. You can ask questions but don't stare like we are walking around with three heads (even if we did have 3 heads).

I have seen this happen when I told people I had 2 kids with C.F. The first thing they did was to look at them and then talk like they weren't there while staring at them constantly. On the opposite side of the spectrum, when I tell people I have M.S. and because I don't always use a walker or wheelchair doesn't mean I feel good when I walk. I still try to do my own grocery shopping and recently while I was on the checkout line, I let the cashier know that I have M.S. and without going on about my limitations, I asked if I could get someone to bag my groceries. Most times, they cooperate without the stares I sometimes get, knowing they think I was just being lazy. Like I said, just because I'm not using a walking device doesn't mean I don't need help. I sometimes find them getting an attitude.

I have relapsing/remitting M.S. I have some good days and some bad. I tend to drop things easily and by the time I am done shopping, I am ready to collapse so trying to pack my bags could be a long process for me. This time, the kid who packed the groceries crammed so much stuff in the bags that a weight lifter probably couldn't have carried them. I know some kids and adults that have never been affected with bad health usually take for granted that everyone is capable of doing such tasks with ease. It is not always that way for everyone. Please have some understanding without us going into our whole life story and take what we say for value.

On another occasion, while taking my son to get his learner's permit, after handing the woman his birth certificate and other proofs of identification, the woman reading the information said he couldn't possibly be old enough to drive even though it was the day of his eighteenth birthday and I (his mother) was with him with my own I.D. So what should have been a perfect day for him ended up making him feel bad because of his small size. As an adult, after the woman at the DMV was given all of our I.D.'s, should have kept her mouth shut instead of me having to explain that my son had Cystic Fibrosis and most have problems with their weight and size. Then, she felt bad but after a while, I get sick and tired of explaining myself.

ME AND MY TWO SONS DANNY AND DONNIE: LAST FAMILY
PICTURE BEFORE LOSING BROTHER MARC AND THEIR DAD

Chapter 23

MY OTHER KIDS

I WOULD ALSO LIKE TO DISCUSS my other children. They are now twenty-five and thirty-two years old. Their names are Don and Dan. Though neither 2 of these kids had Cystic Fibrosis like their brother and sister, they too have suffered. They were the middle children between my other two kids who had the disease. When they were younger, I had to spend a lot of time with Meg and Marc through doctor visits, hospitalizations, medicine times, special cooked meals to help Meg and Marc gain weight (including allowing my 2 kids who suffered from C.F. to pretty much eat whatever they liked). Because of trying to help them gain weight, they could eat anything they wanted. At this time, my other two children had issues with gaining too much weight. I am sure they felt left out. I feel bad for them and I hope to God they understand they are loved just as much as Meg and Marc were. I also pray that they grow from this as I see them both doing the best they can and while working with what they had to deal with. I think they both turned out pretty well though they, like most teens, were difficult and they had a lot to deal with. I want you guys to know how very proud I am of you both. I know this has been hard for you and I hope you can understand I am with you and so is God. I love you guys!

Chapter 24

REFLECTIONS

I HAVE SPOKEN THROUGHOUT THIS BOOK on many subjects from my own beginning to the lives and deaths of many close to me, the natural and supernatural. I hope I have been able to reach many through my words and experiences. I am sure for those of you that really know me can see that within these pages, I speak from my within my inner being. I don't have all of the answers only to what I have seen and been through. I truly believe that God has guided my hand through what I wrote. I am sure he has made what I've gone through both good and bad and to be able to express through my writing to him. I give thanks to him for allowing me to go beyond the blind spots of life and to see clearer into his world and the world to come. Though I have cried throughout my life, I am still able to smile and to look at life's adversities and still go on despite my losses to teach others to keep going no matter what happens and for me to continue to grow thru life's lessons.

To the people who have never met me, I hope you are able to be open to what I have written and believe there is more to life than what the physical eye can see or the mind can comprehend. Also, to people who thought they knew me and what I was about, they too may be surprised by the fact that I have gone through more than they knew before I wrote this book.

Throughout my life, I have joked around a lot and have been probably on several occasions misunderstood, especially while I went through my heavy drinking episodes and acted like a fool at times, but the real me is the one who is writing this book.

In this past year of August 2006, I got into an accident that I myself caused because of my drinking and almost killed myself trying to suppress my emotions and feelings. Trust me; I look at that accident as mixed blessings. It made me see that drinking and driving don't mix. I would never do that again not only because the law says it's wrong but because it is wrong! I thank God I didn't kill anyone else. I broke several ribs and received another head injury. Dealing with M.S. is enough and I don't need any more problems. I know a lot of you out there, people I know personally who have DWI's, still drive to the bars. If you want to drink, it's your business but getting behind the wheel after drinking equals you sitting behind the wheel of a loaded cannon. The person is the one loaded and the car is ready to damage anything in its path. It's not worth it, wake up and be responsible because you should think of others for once in your lives. If you want to keep drinking, call a cab. It's a lot cheaper than courts, lawyers, and possibly the penalties within the new laws which may be much tougher even without hurting anyone. You need to think about yourself. If you need help, ask for it. It doesn't make you less of a person to admit that you need help. I used to think it was a weak person who had to run to someone else to sort out their problems but then I realized how many people would come to me and ask advice. Then, I realized there was a time that I needed to seek help too! It is allowed. So, go for it. My new motto is: Live, Love, Go for It (as long as it doesn't hurt anyone else).

Chapter 25

ANGELS AMONG US

I TRULY BELIEVE IN ANGELS AND their guidance throughout our lives. In almost everything that has happened in my own life since I was 3 years old, I've personally felt the power of angels.

I remember when I was a little girl dreaming of cherubs and flying with them. To this day, I am a collector of angels and I believe angels walk among us. Some of them take human form from anything from a derelict on the street to a person in a 3 piece suit. I have felt their warnings on several occasions. Some people may call it psychic abilities but I believe it is the power of angels.

When I was a child, I remember stories my parents would tell me of encounters they and other members of my family had with angels. One of the stories was when I was sick in the hospital, like I spoke of in an earlier chapter when I was 9 years old. At one point, I had slipped into a coma and my parents had gone to our church where my dad worked and went to the altar to pray with our minister for me to be healed. After leaving the church, my parents drove to the hospital and they both heard a voice telling them I was alright and when they arrived at the hospital, they found out that I had come out of my coma.

Another encounter occurred before my daughter had been diagnosed with Cystic Fibrosis. I was praying for an answer and that's when I picked up Dr. Spock's baby book and automatically turned to the chapter on Cystic Fibrosis. Then, in 1992, I had 2 near misses in possible car accidents and then, within days, I had been hit by someone who went through a red light. I felt after that accident, I was being warned of the accident that would nearly take my own life. The positive thing that came out of this accident was that my son (who was 3 years old at the time) was not in the car with me even though he was supposed to be. Something told me not to bring him that day. If I did bring him, he most likely would have been killed as his car seat was in the car and broke during my car accident and it hit me in the head. Ironically, I was on the way to walk someone's dog (one of the things I did for a living), when the phone rang. On the phone was my minister asking me to mail something to him which made me run late so I decided not to bring the baby with me. Thank God I didn't bring him!

In August of 2006, I had another almost fatal accident and had 2 warnings within that week prior to this time.

Last but not least, I believe I met face to face with an angel who turned to me in a local bar and basically told me to stop drinking and that it was ruining my life and he said to me you know who I am and who sent me to you, but I didn't, as I never met him before. He also stated he was a messenger, and I know he was an angel. It actually was ruining my life. You can drink but don't make it an everyday habit or the most important thing in your life.

My children all had imaginary friends. My daughter's friend was Aunt Gretchen, my son Donnie's was Zeke, my son Danny's was Anne Marie, and Marc's was Jim and Frank. I believe they were my kids' guardian angels. I am adding this page several years after writing my book. I will explain more in my second book entitled, "Racing Hondas in Heaven". Since I wrote this book six years has passed, now my son Marc also has died from Cystic Fibrosis on February 2, 2011 so I feel he deserved his own book, as I have so much more to tell you.

THE NIGHT MARC PASSED I believe that if we all just took the time to listen to those internal messages when we feel something is wrong, we would then understand that we all have our own guardian angels watching over us.

AFTERWORD

Venting Through Poetic Expression

(I have written these poems to deal with the loss of my children)

THE TWILIGHT OF MY LIFE:

<u>Written by Peggy S Imm-Anesi</u>

Another year has passed; I am now another year older
As my years have increased I find myself bolder
To be true to myself before I can be true to all others
During the years I was a daughter, a wife then a Mother
Oh, yes there were many trials along the way
But each night my eyes would close and I would think of each day
What I did right or what I did wrong
Sometimes the day felt it could be written in a sad song
Other days would be like the sunshine of my life
By the people I would meet with their
smiles, I could fly high like a kite
But now I am older and in life have learned many things

But in the end my friends we will be alone
until our heavenly bell rings
What I have learned is to respect myself
now and that is the right thing.
We all do good and sometimes we do bad
I am choosing the good so I am not sad,
If people decide to walk through their life now without me
I will accept that in my Twilight years and just like another song
Just let it be.
If I have learned anything in life is that I am important too
And from that, I take a vow to myself, as God made only **one** you.

It's not how long you live it
is what you do with it

We are born as humans with a body and a soul
We learn too quickly that we will all eventually grow old
We all need to grow in spirit while here in our own way
Hopefully while we are here can smile at least once every day.
There will be times our tears may come pouring down
So try and replace those tears with a smile, instead of a frown
We all face trials and tribulations in our lives
But the bottom line is: you are the only one that can change
what you do to make the most from this thing we called life.

WHY DO PEOPLE PRETEND TO CARE WHEN THEY DON'T?

Why do people pretend to care when they don't even have a clue
I think because if they really walked in my
shoes, they wouldn't know what to do.
We all have a cross or two to bear in this
thing called life for the most part
But I get so feed up when so many give advice
and think they are so very smart.
Unless you have been through the things that life has handed me
Only then can I listen to you and feel your
words and that will set us both free
To understand why my heart cries the way that
it does when I write the things I wrote
And if you went through what I have been through
we would only then be in the same boat.
So the next time you try and offer me some good advice
Unless you have experienced the things I have, you
need to stop for 1 minute and really think twice.
We all have to handle things in our own way
So let me do what I do so I can live another day.

To Those Who Don't Get Me

I have been asked time and time again to go
on and forget the ones that are gone
But a mother who has lost two kids will always have that bond.
When you give birth to children you will
always be connected by your soul
And that is why, my friends that I make our story told
Meg and Marc's lives were cut short never to have grown old
But they both lived long enough for us to
know they were both so very bold
Do you ever ask yourselves what you
would do if this happen to you?
Only then I would be sure you would
understand why I do what I do.
Just because someone leaves this world and dies
My children are still in my heart and I continue
to picture them through my eyes.
They were both real as real could be and
then they met their final destiny
Though no longer here their memories will still live on
And I will keep them alive through me as I am still their Mom.

Thoughts

Everyday is a gift, that is why it is called the present
Smile much, laugh out loud tell a joke or two
Shake someone's hand, offer someone help
It doesn't cost anything to be kind to people
We all have our crosses to bear and it is not easy some days
Grow from the pain within you and make
others' lives easier by listening
Without offering advice as sometimes that is
all anyone needs as we all need to vent.
The rewards fill the soul plentiful and
Everyone comes out a winner.

GOING ON WITH LIFE

Waking up is so hard for me just about everyday
Since my Meg and Marc left me and went away.
Your smiles, your humor, your practical jokes is all so missed
I could say more but it would fill the world's biggest list.
Then again when everything is said and done
If I could make a wish is again to be with my son.
I lost a daughter too with her eyes so bright
When I look up at the stars in the sky I see her beauty in night
I know we will be together someday when the time is right.
Hugs and kisses when I arrive will be in tall order
I miss you two so very much… my precious
son and my beautiful daughter.

JUST LET ME BE ME

I write this for my two children Meg and
Marc who are no longer with me
A mothers' grieving is so different from others
we lose, as strong as they may be.
It never goes away it stays with you all
the time never to set you free
My son Marc's room is still the way it was
the day he left it, exactly the same
With all of his stuff like pictures and clothes and
trophies which were his tickets to fame.
The only thing different behind that closed door
Is Marc himself of which is now a memory
in my eyes need I say more?
My grief is still strong for my kids that are now gone
My precious baby boy and his big sister
but our bond remains strong.
I was with them both from the beginning until the end
And that is what makes a Mom different from all of their friends.
Meg's logo was "No Fear" as that was on her car all of
the time and Marc's is "LNR" which is now on mine.
The stickers on cars represent his memory for family
and friends his memory lives on as there is no end...

FOR MY TWO OTHER
SONS DON AND DAN

I have lost two of the four of my pride and joy in life
Let me start at the beginning when I
became their father Don's wife.
I thought life would be filled we a happy and a wonderful ending
But then came a illness CF with a death
sentence from the beginning.
It robbed my family of so much in life
and ours became a life of strife
To Meg and Marc who suffered the torture and the pain
Then their two brothers Don and Dan at times
watched it without going insane.
My two other children lost out on so much but one
thing for sure always had as much of my love though
they may not realize it as life was so tough
I feel for the two of them who stood by the wayside so many times
As I was running with the other two to Doctors
and Hospitals, life was not kind.

I want to say now to my sons Donnie and Danny
I promise to love you both as much as I can
as my love for you in my heart
Is all so plenty
I am sorry you both had to go through this with me losing Meg,
Marc and also your Daddy. Love you guys so much! Mom

WE ALL NEED TO GIVE
SOMETHING TO THE WORLD

I truly believe we all have our own special gift to give to mankind
Now by writing my books I have finally found mine.
Life gives us pain and all so much sorrow
But then again we can always hope there will be a better tomorrow.
We are born, we grow, we learn, make
mistakes we laugh and we play
Then we grow older with each passing day.
Take from what you have been through and do something well
Though at times how well I know life can be Hell.
My strength I know comes from the one
who hung for us on the cross
And if you think about he should be looked
up to as the one and only boss
He died for us all without blinking an eye
And he waits with open arms for who
believe in him high in the sky
He is the one who has inspired me to write
and to hopefully help the lost souls
As I know he wants great things from us so
we can all continue to stand tall.

HAPPY TIMES ON VACATION AT SEASIDE
WITH DON AND THE BOYS

www.ingramcontent.com/pod-product-compliance
Lightning Source LLC
Chambersburg PA
CBHW030342290526
45785CB00004B/1570